Renewals: 020 7307 2365   Email: library@fra.ac.uk

in a week

SUE CAVE

Hodder & Stoughton

A MEMBER OF THE HODDER HEADLINE GROUP

00001917

As the champion of management, the Chartered Management Institute shapes and supports the managers of tomorrow. By sharing intelligent insights and setting standards in management development, the Institute helps to deliver results in a dynamic world.

chartered

management

institute

inspiring leaders

For more information call 01536 204222 or visit www.managers.org.uk

Orders: please contact Bookpoint Ltd, 130 Milton Park, Abingdon, Oxon OX14 4SB. Telephone: (44) 01235 827720, Fax: (44) 01235 400454. Lines are open from 9.00–6.00, Monday to Saturday, with a 24 hour message answering service. Email address: orders@bookpoint.co.uk

British Library Cataloguing in Publication Data
A catalogue record for this title is available from The British Library

ISBN 0 340 849711

First published   2001
Impression number   10 9 8 7 6 5 4 3 2 1
Year   2007 2006 2005 2004 2003 2002

Typeset by SX Composing DTP, Rayleigh, Essex.
Printed in Great Britain for Hodder & Stoughton Educational, a division of Hodder Headline Plc, 338 Euston Road, London NW1 3BH by Cox & Wyman Ltd, Reading, Berkshire

CONTENTS

WITHDRAWN

■ I N T R O D U C T I O N ■

We should all be interested in consumer behaviour, simply because we are all consumers. This is an activity that goes on constantly throughout our lives, and affects the way we think, the way we feel, the way we look, and how we spend our time. A large number of us also provide services or products to consumers. We then need to understand, from a wider perspective than our own, what influences consumer behaviour and how best to present our products.

In this book, you will find a brief introduction to basic psychological processes, attitudes towards money, purchasing behaviour, different types of consumer, the branding, advertising and retailing of products, and negative effects of consumerism.

Each day is broken down into topics, which are outlined at the start. Each topic is then presented in the form of definitions/issues, important points and implications. There are also some activities for you to try. A summary is given to recap at the end of each day.

Know Your Consumer I: Basic Psychological Processes

Today you will be focusing on the psychological processes that underpin consumer behaviour. It is essential to understand these if you want to develop successful products and market them effectively. The processes that we will examine today are:

- perception and attention
- learning and memory
- motivation
- attitudes and attitude change
- the self-concept
- group processes.

Perception and attention

Definitions/issues
Attention is the process through which we become consciously aware of stimulation received from our surroundings. Clearly, we encounter a massive amount of information, and cannot attend to it all, therefore we have to be selective. Perception is the interpretation we place on that input. Objects and situations will be perceived in very different ways by different people as a result of these processes.

Important points about attention
1   We process information quite rapidly, but there is a limit to how quickly we can do this.

2 We can generally only deal with one item or activity at a time, unless we are well-practised or items are presented to different senses (eg, we can read a book and listen to music at the same time).

3 Choice of item to attend to depends on what is important to us, either in the short or the long term.

4 Importance may be determined by our motives or by other factors such as novelty and distinctiveness.

Implications

- Avoid presenting too much information at any one time ('advertising clutter').
- Use as many senses (eg vision, hearing) as possible to put information across.
- Find out what is important to consumers.
- Make products and advertisements novel and distinctive.

Important points about perception

1 Perception is a constructive process rather than a mechanical registration of 'reality'.
2 The constructions that we build are based on previous experience, expectations and motivation.
3 Although there will be broad similarities, there will also be differences between individuals in the perceptions they construct.
4 The more ambiguous the input received, the more constructions and interpretations will differ in different people.

Implications

- Basic messages need to be clear and unambiguous to the intended recipients.
- It is important to identify the target group for any communications in order to achieve this.
- Some ambiguity can be useful to create interest.
- Objects and messages can be used as symbols for other things, or to evoke fantasies or memories.

Learning and memory

Definitions/issues

Learning is a relatively permanent change in behaviour that is the result of experience. Changes induced by drugs, injury or ageing are excluded by this definition. Memory is the storage of information about these experiences within the individual and its retrieval from the memory stores. These processes are important in determining how long-lasting influences on our behaviour will be.

Important points about learning

1 Learning is more likely if experiences are repeated.
2 Learning can occur through the **association** of two events eg if they are presented close together in time.
3 Learning depends on **reinforcement**: behaviours which lead to pleasant consequences are more likely to be repeated.
4 Learning can occur through the **observation** and **imitation** of the experiences of others as well as through personal experience.
5 Some people are more likely to be imitated than others.

Implications

- People need to encounter products and advertisements as often as possible (don't overdo this, though, as it can lead to 'advertising wearout').
- Presenting a product alongside something that is

- already regarded highly will enhance the esteem in which it is held.
- Purchasing must lead to a perception of pleasant consequences if it is to be repeated.
- The reports obtained from other people, by word of mouth or through promotions and advertisements, have a significant effect on behaviour.
- People on whom we model ourselves will make the best promoters of products.

Important points about memory

1 Memory consists of both a short-term and a long-term store; not all information received gets passed on to the long-term store.
2 Information is more likely to reach the long-term store if it is repeated, vivid, personally relevant, and if it is processed in terms of meaning rather than just looked at superficially.
3 Information that fits in well with our existing interests will be better remembered because it can be slotted into the way we have organised our memory store.
4 Recall is a process of reconstructing the past, and may well be distorted.

Implications

- Product information needs to be repeated, personalised and to 'make people think' (eg by being presented in an incomplete form) if it is to be stored in memory for any length of time.
- Elaboration of information or products in the form of visual images, jingles or distinctive packaging will

assist memory processes.
- Products and information must be made relevant to the interests of consumers, or interest must be created by the products.
- Key information must be presented clearly so that it will be remembered accurately; what is implied may be remembered as factual.

Motivation

Definition/issues

Motivation is the energising force which drives behaviour and sustains it until some goal is reached. It involves a state of **need** and goal-directed behaviour aimed at satisfying the need. Motives may be learnt or unlearnt, positive (desire for something) or negative (desire to avoid something) and conscious or unconscious. Since they make us behave in particular ways, it is important to understand what motives we have and how these can be developed.

Important points

1 **Biological** motives such as the need for food are common to everybody; there are, however, differences in the way that people prefer to satisfy them.
2 We also have **cognitive** motives, such as the needs for stimulation, consistency and beauty.
3 **Social** motives include the need for positive regard from others, the need to belong to groups, the need for power and the need to achieve and fulfill our aspirations.
4 **Frustration** of our needs (when efforts to reach goals are seen to be blocked) is a powerful influence on behaviour.
5 Behaviour is also determined by **values,** or overriding

principles; these vary according to the individual and according to culture.

Implications

- Product marketers need to find out how different groups of people prefer to satisfy their biological needs.
- Both products themselves and advertisements can capitalise on the cognitive needs such as the need for beauty in our surroundings.
- Products and advertisements can be created to appeal to our aspirations and linked with membership of desirable social groups.
- Products which offer ways of overcoming frustrations (real or manufactured) will also be regarded highly.
- The values of the target group need to be established in order to develop the right approach to marketing.
- Symbolism in advertisements may be used to appeal to unconscious motives (sexual, for example).

Attitudes and attitude change

Definition/issues
An attitude is a lasting general evaluation of an object, person or issue; a like or a dislike. According to the widely accepted ABC model, it has three components:

- **affective**: a feeling or emotional response towards the attitude object;
- **behavioural**: a predisposition towards certain behaviours with respect to the attitude object;

- **cognitive:** a set of beliefs and knowledge about the object concerned.

Our attitudes towards products and services are obviously important determinants of whether or not we will purchase them, and a prime reason for advertising is to change attitudes.

Important points

1 People like to maintain consistency between attitudes towards different, related objects and issues; they also like to maintain consistency between the components of a given attitude. Inconsistency creates tension and is a force for attitude change. The level of tension depends on the importance of the issue.
2 Attitudes towards a product will be determined by the combination of attitudes towards different attributes of that product, eg the cost and speed of a car.
3 Existing attitudes are important determinants of whether or not people will accept new information.
4 Social norms and the perceived consequences of purchase also contribute towards our attitudes to a product.
5 The process of changing attitudes must take into account several elements of the communication employed, such as the communicator, content of the message and the nature of the recipient.

- If people can be shown to be inconsistent in their attitudes or persuaded to change one component this will create pressure to change. Persuading green consumers that it is important to recycle as well as to conserve energy is an example of the first; presenting new information about a product (cognitive change) or persuading them to try a sample (behavioural change) is an example of the second.

- It is essential to build on existing attitudes rather than challenging these at the outset.
- Market research needs to take into account several different attributes of a product if it is to develop products that more closely approximate consumers' ideals.
- It may be more appropriate to manipulate or appeal to social norms to produce attitude change rather than targeting individuals (as in the anti smoking campaign).
- The communicator's credibility and image must be suited to the product and the target group.
- The most effective messages in general are those which present both sides of an argument, repeat the main points and employ a moderate level of fear (if appropriate).

Implications

Self concept

Definition/issues

Self concept is an organised set of perceptions about the self – it is what we think we are like rather than what we are like. It is important to our discussion of consumer behaviour because we will buy products that fit in with our view of ourselves; we also use some products to relieve our insecurities about ourselves.

ACTIVITY

You can investigate your own self concept by answering the question 'Who am I'? Try to write down 20 responses to the question. When you have done this, look at the different types of attribute you have written down.

Important points

1 The self concept consists of three components:
   – **self image** (this includes personality traits, abilities, social roles, attitudes, motivations, and body image)
   – **self esteem** (how much we value ourselves)
   – **ideal self** (the person we would like to be).
2 The self concept is mostly social in origin and derives from the feedback we receive from others about how they perceive us.
3 Another important source of ideas is the social comparisons we make between ourselves and others.
4 The products and services that we consume (eg cars, houses, clothing) can also provide us with ideas about who we are (our **extended self**).
5. The self concept incorporates our gender roles as well as the other roles we play as part of our everyday life (eg father).
6. The **body image** – our ideas about our own body and what we see as ideal – is just as likely to be inaccurate as our ideas about our psychological attributes.

Implications

- The products we buy will be used by others to evaluate us.
- Product attributes need to match some aspect of our self image or our ideal self.
- Products can be used as gifts or self-gifts to boost self-esteem ('you deserve it').
- Products are often sex-typed, ie associated with one sex only, to fit in with gender roles.
- Changing gender roles may necessitate or permit changes in advertising, eg male perfumes.
- Products for the body can take advantage of perceived imperfections or can focus on image as an indicator of group membership, eg fashion.

Group processes

Definitions/issues

This refers to the behaviours we demonstrate which are primarily the result of belonging to social groups. Very few people do not belong, or aspire, to at least one social group. Such groups can exert a powerful influence on behaviour, as anyone who has tried to go against their expectations will confirm, and this influence extends to consumer behaviour.

Important points

1 Social **roles** and **norms** set the standards for behaviours that are expected of people in particular positions in society (roles) or who are members of particular groups (norms).
2 Occupying multiple roles or being in several groups means that there are often conflicting expectations.
3 Group membership is an indicator of status and class: our position in society relative to other people. Consider the implications of belonging to a golf club!
4 We also aspire to belong to certain groups (**reference groups**) which influences our consumption patterns.
5 The family is probably the most important group that most people belong to.
6 The culture we live in also has common ways of behaving which may be deeply ingrained.
7 Nevertheless, there is a variety of alternative lifestyles available in modern society, with correspondingly different patterns of consumption.

Implications

- Standards for behaviour extend to consumption and can be used to sell products, eg executive cars.
- Role conflict provides marketing opportunities as in the development of the convenience food market for the working mother.
- Products need to have a status and identity linked with social groups if they are to transfer those to the consumer.
- The stage a consumer has reached in terms of the family life cycle needs to be taken into account when establishing disposable income and consumer needs.
- Cultural differences are crucial to marketers: selling items that are not part of an established way of life is likely to be an uphill struggle.
- The lifestyle of the target group of consumers needs to be established accurately before products can be successfully developed and marketed.

Summary

Today you have looked at some basic psychological processes which are crucial to understanding consumer behaviour:

- Attracting the attention of consumers and influencing the way they perceive the information presented.
- Ensuring that the information presented is learnt and can be recalled.
- The motives, needs and values of target consumers must

be researched so that product development is appropriate to them.

- Attempts at producing attitude change can focus on information, emotion or behaviour – but must take into account existing attitudes, social norms and the nature of the communicator, message and recipient.
- Linking products with the self concept of consumers is an important feature of marketing; this has been particularly the case with sex-typed products and those linked with body image.
- Group membership creates expectations which extend to consumption of certain products or services.

Tomorrow we shall move on to examine the way that consumers think about money - and parting with it!

Know Your Consumer II: Attitudes to Money

The ultimate aim of consumer research is to encourage
people to spend money on particular products in preference
to others. In order to do this, it is important understand how
people feel about money and to look at differences in
spending patterns. Today's topics address these issues in the
following ways:

- Psychology of money, economics and pricing
- Poverty and wealth
- Spending, saving and borrowing
- Targeting those with resources.

Psychology of money, economics and pricing

Definitions/issues
In modern societies, money (coins, notes, cheques and credit
cards) is the way that we exchange our work for the goods
and services we want, save for future needs or speculate in
the hope of making more money.

Important points
1 Money means different things to different people; those
   who are employed may see it as a good thing whilst the
   unemployed see it as a source of worry and its absence as
   shameful. Males associate money with competence,
   financial risk-taking and management whereas females see
   it as a means of obtaining goods and enjoyable
   experiences.

2 The worth of different types of money may not be accurately interpreted. A coin will be seen as having less value than a note of the same denomination. Credit cards are seen as less 'real' than cash.

3 Money also has a symbolic value representing power, security, happiness and satisfaction. It is not generally acceptable as a gift (except from parents to children) since it symbolises status and seniority.

4 Expenditure on goods and services depends less on how much money we have than on how well-off we feel and what we think is likely to happen in the future. Our current income determines expenditure on food and other consumables whereas durables such as cars and major appliances are more influenced by **consumer confidence** about the future.

5 'Spenders' are generally healthier, happier and more optimistic than self-deniers. The money-troubled are more dissatisfied with life, themselves and their relationships.

6 A fair exchange is expected when purchases are made.

Consumers have an idea about an **acceptable price range** and products must fall within that to be considered for purchase. They also have a **reference price** which is the price they expect to pay for a particular product based on fairness or past price.

7 For many products price is also considered to be an indicator of the quality of the goods. Although this **market belief** is not always justified, it is a good guideline.

8. Despite this, consumers' knowledge of prices is often poor, especially for some categories of goods, eg coffee.

ACTIVITY

Jot down some items that you buy regularly. Note alongside each what you think the price is. Next time you make a purchase, check your estimates to see if you are exactly right, within 10% or outside that range. Which types of item were correct and which were incorrect?

Implications

- It is important to understand the subjective value that money has for your target consumers. If you want to persuade them to make purchases they must feel that they are getting value for money.
- Coins and credit cards may be used more readily than notes.
- Since money is not acceptable as a gift, goods and services can be marketed as alternatives.

- Measurement of consumer confidence is an important part of marketing. Questions such as 'do you feel better or worse financially than you did a year ago?' and 'how well-off do you expect to be in a year's time?' can be used to measure this.
- Marketing strategy can be adapted to current economic conditions. For example, Campbell's Soup Co. responded to a recession by putting soup into family size tins and cutting prices after discovering that more people were having to eat at home. They also marketed soups as sauces for home cooking.
- When new lines are introduced, products must be priced within the acceptable price range. There are exceptions: eg Dualit toasters priced at £100 compared to the usual range of £12–30. Marketed as catering equipment, they are stylish and indicate status and seriousness about cooking.
- Offering goods at prices that are too low may in some cases affect sales adversely as it raises doubts about quality. In one case a new cheap range of cosmetics failed to sell until the price was increased. Low-priced goods need to undermine the perception that price is associated with quality. Using quality brand names, selling in quality stores, offering warranties and employing advertisements can be used to achieve this. Konica films used the slogan 'Why pay the price if you can't see the difference?' to attract buyers away from the more expensive Kodak films.

Poverty and wealth

Definitions/issues
Poverty can be defined absolutely in terms of total earnings below the amount required for maintenance of physical and mental health. It can also be defined in terms of the 10% of the population who earn the least. Wealth is objectively defined (eg by the Inland Revenue) on the basis of income. Subjectively most people define a wealthy person as one who has substantial savings and a lot of property rather than just a high income.

Important points
1 Research into the culture of poverty has shown that the poor have a **present time orientation**, meaning that short-term goals and gratification will be more important than any long-term plans. Risk-taking behaviours will be reduced.

ACTIVITY

Before you read on, look at the reasons for poverty given below and see which you agree with:

• Laziness	45%
• Chronic unemployment	42%
• Drink	40%
• Ill health	36%
• Too many children	31%
• Old age and loneliness	30%
• Lack of education	29%
• Lack of foresight	21%
• Deprived childhood	16%

(The percentages given show the number of people in Britain endorsing that explanation; other European countries showed a different pattern of responses)

2 **Just world beliefs** mean that rather than blaming society, the poor are generally seen as responsible for their own fate. Such beliefs would lead to agreement with statements such as: 'In this country almost everyone can make it if they try hard enough' and 'most people on social security are lazy'.

3 A large proportion of wealth is concentrated in the hands of a relatively small number of people. In America, the wealthiest 20% have 50% of the income. Most people see this as unfair and consider the rich to be overpaid and the poor to be underpaid. There is also a **preference drift effect** whereby people consider their own standard of living as the minimum acceptable.

ACTIVITY

Indicate the 6 most important reasons, in order of importance, why you think some people are better off financially than others. When you have finished, compare your answers with those given below.

4 As with poverty, people offer many explanations for wealth. Most British people see the wealthy as having been lucky or helped by others (eg through inheritance or good schooling) rather than as having worked harder. Thus the poor are responsible for their condition but the rich are not. Richer people are also judged to have other positive

attributes such as being more likeable and attractive.

5 Although most people would like to be wealthy there is no
   evidence that wealth is associated with happiness; it simply
   seems to change the nature of the person's worries. Some
   research indicates that those who live in advanced market
   democracies may experience more material satisfaction, but
   they are increasingly unhappy. Cultural values in many of
   these societies seem to be moving towards the pursuit of
   spiritual development rather than material gain.

6 The wealthy spend more money on services, travel and
   investment. They do not buy home furnishings,
   appliances, etc because they are generally older than the
   less wealthy and already have those items. Newly wealthy
   people, such as lottery winners, spend money on things
   such as property, cars, consumer durables and travel. Most
   do not continue to work and they will also invest most of
   their new wealth.

Implications

- Products which target the poor need to cater for short-term needs rather than long-term goals; any investments need to be low-risk.
- The different images held by most people about the nature of rich and poor people – and the reasons for their financial condition – mean that very few will want to be seen as poor. Wherever possible, people will tend to consume in ways which put them in a positive light and make them feel better about themselves. For example, in '*The Road to Wigan Pier*' George Orwell notes that the poor people he encountered would purchase relatively expensive 'luxury' foods such as chocolate biscuits and condensed milk for these very reasons.
- Appealing to the new urge for spiritual development rather than associating products with purely material aims or even with happiness may be more successful with modern consumers.
- Products which target the wealthy need to emphasise investment and provide services. Different types of wealthy people exist and to some extent they will be interested in different products.

Targeting those with resources

Definitions/issues

'It is much easier to hit a bull's eye when you can see the target'. This means that it is important to identify the people who have money (economic resources) and the time to spend it (time resources) since they will make more likely consumers than those who do not. How they are spending that money must also be identified.

Important points

1 Economic resources are identified by looking at family income. Since the early decades of the twentieth century there has been an increase in the proportion which is spent on housing and a decrease in the amount spent on food and clothing; consequently more is left over for spending on other commodities.

2 Expenditure on food and other consumables is largely determined by current income, with expenditure on durables being more affected by consumer confidence.

3 Age is another important determinant: housing is the main expenditure for the 35–44 year-old group; eating out and clothes for the 45–54 group; and health care for the 65+ group.

4 The **'up market'** is the top 25% income group, typically dual-income households who are time constrained and emphasise quality when purchasing goods or services. They buy furniture, electronic goods, tableware, tools, building materials, fine jewellery and menswear. This group is print-oriented ie they read newspapers and magazines rather than watch television.

5 The super-affluent group at the top end of the scale have most appliances and home furnishings already. They spend more on services such as education, travel, nannies and cleaners.

6 The **'down market'** comprises the majority of consumers world-wide. In the USA this group comprises the young, old, single and divorced consumers. They spend highly on education, prescription drugs, tobaccco, milk and laxatives

but are light users of products such as wine and Diet Pepsi.

7 The availability of credit may extend resources temporarily but in the long term they will be reduced because credit costs money. Young consumers and those with high incomes may be more inclined to borrow and people are most likely to borrow to finance education, medical bills and cars.

8 Many people feel that they do not have enough time, known as being '**time crunched**' which indicates that time is another valuable resource to consider. People have time budgets and 38% will go without sleep to try and fit in more activities. About half of the Americans surveyed indicate that they would forgo a day's pay in order to have more time with family and friends. Women, parents and minorities are the most time-crunched groups.

9 As well as working time we have **leisure time** – that time during which we have a choice about our activities – and **obligated time** which is not discretionary, involving housework, personal care and socialising.

Fred was feeling time crunched...

Implications

- Knowledge of the way the income is apportioned between different areas of expenditure can be used to guide marketing strategies.
- Measures of consumer confidence can be used to forecast future demand for some goods and to plan levels of production and stocking.
- Age and income are a useful guide to the type of product and service likely to be of interest to different groups.
- The 'up market' group require quality goods and services. They are generally short of time, and will pay more for goods that are immediately available, trouble-free and where customer care is of a high standard, limiting inconvenience. Being older they are also a good market for products and services aimed at enhancing youth and health such as beauty products and health clubs. Since they have desirable property, security systems and insurances are also likely to be of interest.
- The 'down market' represent a sizeable proportion of consumers, particularly for certain types of product. They respond to marketing strategies which offer 'no frills' but still provide a stylish retail environment and treat customers with respect. 'Successful discounters have made their mark by convincing customers that they are smart and special, not poor riff-raff'. The Aldi chain of supermarkets offers low prices, a restricted range of products, charges for bags and provides a minimum of service.

- Time crunched individuals will be less willing to spend time making purchasing decisions and shopping. Making these activities easier by providing information about products, building out-of-town shopping malls so that parking is less problematic, easing congestion and queues in stores, making provision for mail-order and internet shopping, accepting different forms of payment and reducing the likelihood of post-purchase problems will all assist consumers to make their purchases speedily and efficiently.
- Obligated time can be reduced by selling labour-saving devices such as microwave ovens, dishwashers and ready meals. Hiring services such as child care, cleaners and gardeners will also help the time-crunched.
- Where leisure time is reduced it may be more intensively used. Air travel and expensive sports facilties may help such people to make the best use of their time. There may also be a move away from less intensive activities such as golf to more intensive sports such as squash.
- Some products may permit **polychronic time use** where several activities can be carried out simultaneously. Mobile phones and laptops allow people to work while they travel; exercise equipment can be fitted with lecterns so that books can be read whilst exercising.

Summary

Today we have looked at the ways consumers spend money and use their time resources:

- As well as an objective value, money has a subjective and a symbolic value; economic stability is important to mental health and status.
- Current income and consumer confidence about the future are important determinants of both spending and marketing strategies.
- Goods must be priced within the acceptable range for the type of produdct; quality is associated with price so too low a price will be counterproductive.
- The poor want short-term consumable goods and the wealthy services and investments; they both want to enhance their self-esteem through their purchases.
- Up market and down market marketing require different strategies but there may be some overlap.
- The time crunched will respond to products and services which save obligated time, enable better use of leisure time and permit polychronic time use.

Tomorrow we will be looking at how consumers go through the process of purchasing.

Know Your Consumer III: Purchasing

Having established that your consumer will be prepared to part with a certain amount of money the next step is to look at what customers want to buy and how they want to buy it. You also need to consider how they feel afterwards as that will influence future purchases and the recommendations they make to others. Today we will look at:

- Materialism
- Psychology of purchasing
- Decision-making
- Purchasing behaviour

Materialism

Definitions/issues
Materialism can be defined as the desire for money and possessions above everything else. Some possessions are consumable (eg services and perishable goods) but many are not (eg cars, pictures, ornaments, furniture). It is important to understand why people desire durable goods such as these.

Important points
1 Objects may be desired because they have an **instrumental purpose.** They may provide amusement, as in the case of music centres. Ownership of objects may give us a feeling of control over our environment – a trait readily seen in children and one that is particularly important to males.

2 Objects also have a **symbolic purpose**, standing for the personal qualities of the owner and giving us a sense of identity. This seems to be particularly important to females.

3 There are age differences in what is regarded as the favourite possession.

ACTIVITY

Try to remember what your own favourite possession was when you were 5, 10, 15, and 20 years old.

On the whole young children tend to prefer cuddly toys; older children like sports equipment; adolescents prefer musical equipment, cars and jewellery and adults are interested in photographs and jewellery.

4 Males prefer action and leisure-related objects, eg cars. Females favour items which have more social and emotional connotations, eg jewellery.

5 Class differences do not seem to affect the types of possession favoured but there are differences in the reasons given for preferences. Unemployed people are more swayed by emotional and instrumental features of goods. Middle class commuters are more interested in the personal history behind items, which could lead to a preference for possessions such as antique furniture.

Implications

- All types of products need to appeal to both the instrumental and symbolic needs of the prospective purchaser. Consumers will match their own image with that of the product.
- Different cultures will have varying preferences for products and diverse ways of interpreting symbols they present. Products need to be designed with these differences in mind.
- Consumer goods can also be used to compensate for personal inadequacies (**symbolic self-completion**). Suggesting that products will make us feel better about ourselves is one way of appealing to this need.
- Since purchasing is based on perceived needs, such needs must be activated or created in the first instance, eg in-store displays and advertising may boost sales of flagging products which people are not bothering to renew. New product lines may have to be

more pro-active: Reebok trainers created the need for adolescents to have new-style footwear with a particular label attached.

Psychology of purchasing

Definitions/issues
The complexity of consumer behaviour is evident in this section as well. There are several different types of consumption and different psychological theories about the purchasing process. They both have implications for marketing strategies.

Important points
1 The first type of consumption involves important purchases which are usually novel or infrequent. They are described as **high involvement** and include houses, cars and pension schemes.
2 Repetitive consumption is when items are bought frequently. Little conscious thought occurs when making such purchases so they are often described as **low involvement**, eg grocery shopping.
3 **Involuntary consumption** occurs when we have little choice about the purchase or when changing to another source is inconvenient. This includes petrol and banking services.
4 **Group consumption** is defined as being the result of group decisions. For example, the views of different family members may be taken into account when purchasing a holiday.
5 The **cognitive** approach views purchase as being the outcome of a decision-making process involving seeking

Anne felt a spot of involuntary consumption coming on...

and sifting information, evaluation of costs and benefits of the product, consideration of alternatives and a rational choice between them. This is more likely with high involvement products. Most purchases are replacements (eg cars) or additions (eg televisions) so the brand last bought is often the most important determinant of purchase.

6 The **learning theory** approach views purchase as a learned response based on previous rewards in the form of satisfactory outcomes. Pleasant experiences also create good associations with products; a wine associated with a pleasant evening out may well be chosen again. Repeated purchase may then lead to the formation of habits whereby the same choices are made without thinking when confronted with the same situation. This is more likely with repetitive consumption.

7 The **social** approach sees consumption as determined by the influence of other people. This includes beliefs about what 'important' people think about the purchase, the effect of sales staff on behaviour and the notion of fairness in social exchanges making rewards appropriate to costs.

ACTIVITY

Identify some important purchases you have made and some habitual purchases. Which of the three approaches outlined above (cognitive, learning and social) provides the best explanation for your behaviour in each case?

Implications

- First purchasers are a key group because the purchase may establish a habit and determine later purchases even for high involvement products.
- Establishing brand loyalty has important consequences for later buying behaviour (more about this on Thursday).
- Information search may well be curtailed when an adequate option is found in order to save time. Known as **satisficing**, this implies that the order in which options are evaluated is crucial since those considered first have a better chance of being accepted. Products which are more in the public eye are likely to be in this category.
- Distinctive logos and packaging make it more likely that consumers will be cued to purchase by the sight of a product.
- Advertisements, like any reinforcer, lose their ability to affect behaviour after repetition (known as '**wearout**'). They need to be 'rested' for a while to avoid this happening.
- Unpleasant experiences with products (such as odd taste or faults in manufacture) may have a strong

deterrent effect on behaviour for a long period. This can be very costly to the manufacturer.

- The retailing environment can also contribute towards the rewards experienced by purchasing. This can be done through the provision of pleasure (eg free videos on flights) or information (eg about the journey).
- Sales staff can significantly contribute to rewards experienced by consumers and can shape their behaviour in the direction of purchasing; the opinions of others are important reinforcers.
- The notion of a fair exchange means that if consumers are not making large purchases, or are not very committed to a particular purchase, if it is made difficult for them they may readily change their minds. Thus supermarkets which allow those with only a few items to use a 'baskets only' till will have more chance of retaining their custom.

Decision-making

Definitions/issues

If decision-making is a rational process, marketing managers should simply need to focus on providing products which meet the criteria specified by consumers and ensuring that the information about those products is readily available in an understandable form. If it cannot be explained rationally, awareness of biases and emotional and social influences become more relevant to attempts to influence consumer decisions.

Important points

1 Once a need has been recognised, the first stage of decision-making is the **pre-purchase information search**.

This may be based on previous knowledge and experiences, advertisements, consumer reports and talking to others. There is also **ongoing search**, such as browsing, which is carried out regardless of any needs to purchase. Some information-gathering may also be accidental as a result of simple exposure to advertisements.

2 Search varies in terms of how many alternatives are considered, which alternatives are considered (and in which order) and which information sources are consulted.

3 Search is increased when there is high consumer involvement and when the information is readily available. Grocery shopping involves on average only 12 seconds decision-making time for each purchase.

4 Different groups of consumers have been identified who search for varying lengths of time. A study of car purchasers revealed that 32% were moderate searchers, 26% were low and only 5% were high searchers, the remainder being in between. More educated consumers generally have more confidence in their ability to use information effectively. Very knowledgeable and very inexperienced product users are likely to search the least. Search is also dependent on whether shopping is regarded as a pleasure or a chore and the perceived costs and benefits of searching. Older, higher-income groups usually search less.

5 Significant sources of information during search are advertisements (TV advertisements are especially important for information about style and design of outdoor products and small electrical goods); in-store information (including packaging labels, which are particularly important to women and older consumers), salespeople and family/friends.

6 If brands are perceived to be similar and stores are geographically spread out then search will be reduced.

7 The **consideration set** is the set of alternatives from which the consumer will make a choice. This will depend on memory and what is available at the point of purchase. The size of the set varies according to product, one study finding 6.9 for beer and only 2.2 for air freshener.

8 **Evaluative criteria** used to assess alternative brands will include price (often considered to indicate quality), brand name (which can indicate quality or status, as in designer labels) and country of origin (which may have ideological implications to indicate quality). The importance of each will vary according to product and consumer.

Implications

- Since information about products is often acquired passively and then made use of in the pre-purchase search, 'low-dose' advertising over a period of time may prove to have beneficial long-term effects.
- Knowing which brands consumers consider as alternative purchases provides useful information about the competition faced by a given product.
- Information about which stores are visited can be useful when planning distribution and promotional displays.
- Understanding the differences between segments of the populace regarding search can be useful when planning promotion. If high-search segments are more likely to purchase the product then encouraging search by providing information is likely to prove beneficial. Labelling and advertising may

well pay off. Low search groups may be better
targeted by free samples and price cuts.

- Choice of advertising medium depends on the nature
  of the product and the consumer. Salespeople often
  play an essential role in explaining information to the
  consumer and indicating which characteristics of
  products are important when making a decision.
- It is essential to ensure that a product is part of the
  consumer's consideration set or it will not stand a
  chance of being purchased. This can be done by
  advertising (e.g Saab's slogan: 'Most car accidents
  happen in a showroom') or by offering incentives
  such as discounts.
- Understanding the product attributes that are key
  evaluative criteria can provide a basis for product
  development and promotion. Cutoffs (eg acceptable
  price ranges) and priorities for different attributes
  must also be established.

Purchasing behaviour

Definitions/issues

The process of purchasing involves decisions about whether
to buy, what, when and where to buy and how to pay for the
item. The purchasing process may be aborted at any stage as
a result of new information or changing circumstances. There
are also many factors which can promote purchase and this is
where good marketing strategies pay off.

Important points

1 Many purchases are fully planned. This includes high-
  involvement items eg personal computers (88% of

shoppers make planned purchases in this category) and low-involvement items eg groceries (61% of purchases are based on planning in the form of lists and 80% of items on shopping lists are actually purchased). Planned purchases mostly consist of items which are needed and items which there are financial incentives – such as coupons – to purchase. Partially planned purchases involve plans to buy a product but choice of brand is left until the time of purchase. Unplanned purchases may account for up to 50% of purchases in some categories and can be either the result of memory being triggered or true impulse buying where consumers yield to a sudden urge to buy a product.

ACTIVITY

Think about how many of your purchases were planned, partly planned or unplanned on your last shopping trip.

---

2 **Shopping orientation** (attitude towards shopping) varies. Although shopping has been a key leisure activity in the recent past (serving social, informational and other purposes as well as purchasing) it seems that it is now decreasing. This may be due to lack of time, stress or economic considerations: around 20% of the populace actively dislike shopping. General mood at the time of shopping may affect purchase decisions.

3 Price comparisons between stores ('shopping around') are now less frequent. Stores which offer 'Everyday Low Prices' such as Toys 'R' Us are preferred instead. Service and atmosphere are also important features of their success.

4 Store choice depends on the store's **image** (including
   carpeting, lighting, aisle width, music and clientele);
   location; assortment and quality of goods; efficiency of
   sales personnel; and services offered (eg cash machines,
   restaurants).

5 Successful sales staff are those who are high in expertise
   and trustworthiness, knowledgeable about customers and
   their needs, and able to adapt their interaction styles to suit
   the customer they are dealing with. They can be
   additionally motivated by salary and/or commission for
   sales.

6 Sales can be promoted by eye-level displays and displays
   located at the end of aisles and near check-outs. Price
   reductions, coupons, free samples and offers of other
   goods at reduced prices can also boost sales. These are all
   known as **point-of-purchase stimuli.**

7. Direct sales via mail-order, telephone, newspapers and
   electronic media (cable TV and internet) are increasing
   rapidly. This is due to the greater availability of credit
   cards and lifestyle changes such as less time, more traffic
   and queues. Such shoppers tend to be younger, higher
   income, better educated and live in small towns or rural
   areas although there will be variation according to the
   mode of purchase. Internet shoppers (or 'fast laners') now
   consitute 14% of the population in America and tend to be
   in their early twenties. Direct sales purchasers buy mainly
   clothing, home and office equipment and magazines.

Implications

- Planned purchases can be encouraged by creating needs and offering financial incentives such as coupons.
- Since unplanned purchases account for a significant proportion of sales it is important to trigger needs at the point of purchase with displays and information rather than just relying on consumers' existing plans. Partially planned purchases may also be swayed at this time by special displays and promotions.
- Stores need to establish a good image to prevent customers from shopping around. We will return to this topic in more detail on Thursday as there are many aspects to consider. One option is the provision of facilties such as restrooms (rated as influencing store choice by 51% of women).
- Sales staff need to be well-trained and motivated by incentive schemes. These schemes need to be carefully designed to ensure that they attend to customer satisfaction as well as volume of sales. **Relationship marketing** is a term for the process of building up a relationship with customers in order to keep them using the service/product offered.
- Prime in-store displays and price incentives can boost sales considerably, but they can be expensive. Price cuts in particular can lead to retaliation from competitors or stocking up by consumers, which interrupts projected cash flow.
- Many successful marketers are now using some form of direct sales in addition to the traditional methods. In France vending machines are a popular

way of buying Levis, since they can be sold for £6 less than in the shops. Shopping malls sometimes provide some form of entertainment in order to improve the attitude of consumers towards shopping as an experience.

Summary

Today we have established that:

- Products and services must appeal to both the instrumental and symbolic needs of consumers; and that marketing strategy must activate those needs at the time of purchase.
- Habitual behaviour when purchasing can be developed through establishing brand loyalty; where behaviour is not habitual the perceived rewards and costs of purchasing one product rather than another will determine purchase decisions.
- Provision of product information through advertisements, incentives and trial offers plus point-of-purchase stimuli is an essential part of marketing success.
- Choice of retailing method needs to take account of store image, the importance of relationships in marketing and various forms of direct sales.

Tomorrow we will be exploring different types of consumer and how understanding these differences can be put to good use.

Know Your Consumer IV: Different Types of Consumer

We have already seen that all consumers do not behave in the same way. An awareness of these differences – **'market segmentation'** – is essential for effective product development and marketing. The differences we will be exploring today are:

- Age
- Social class
- Culture
- Family and gender
- Lifestyle and attitudes

Age

Definitions/issues

Here we will be concentrating on young people and the elderly as consumers. Young people are defined as those aged up to the mid- to late teens. They are an important market segment because in some countries they account for as much as 50% of the population and they have more spending power than ever before. In 1994 the average 14 year-old had an income of £9.57 per week. Older ('grey') consumers can be defined as those over 50. Their numbers are increasing as people in general live longer (20% of Europeans will be 62+ by the year 2010). They too have more disposable income and more time to spend it as generous pensions and early retirement are available to many.

Important points

1 Children go shopping with their mothers from a very early age and by five they have a good understanding of money. Parents and families are a significant source of consumer information for children.

2 Children primarily buy sweets, snacks, toys, clothes, videos and sports equipment. By the age of seven 90% will have made purchases without parental supervision. Their favourite purchases change from cuddly toys and sports equipment when younger to more clothing, jewellery and music centres when adolescent.

3 Children also have indirect purchasing power as a result of the influence they exert over their parents (often referred to as **'product pestering'**). This may be the result of seeing advertisements or point-of-sale stimuli in the store. Their requests will be met 50% of the time. They may also show preferences for particular retail outlets.

Jim's son soon learnt the art of product pestering

4 By the age of eight most children can distinguish advertisements from TV programmes and have a moderate understanding of the content of advertisements although they can be easily misled. Memory for advertisements improves with age and is enhanced by the use of visually vivid material and slogans.

5 After the 30–49 year-olds, the 50–64 year-olds have the highest weekly expenditure of any age group. Older consumers tend to spend more on drugs and health care, fuel, household supplies, food to be consumed at home, cars and travel.

6 Older consumers may be less mobile than younger, prefer to shop close to home, less inclined to shop around and like shops where they are recognised by staff. They are also keen to buy particular brands especially goods that come with money-back guarantees.

7 They are less inclined to use credit cards and loans than other groups, preferring to keep their excess money in government securities or accounts that yield interest.

8 Older consumers seem to be less willing to complain about products and services, although there is some variation according to the product. They complain the most about cars, groceries, mail order services and appliances.

9 Self-perceived or 'cognitive age' can be a more important determinant of consumer behaviour than actual chronological age. People generally see themselves as being younger than they really are.

10 Negative stereotypes of the elderly in the media and advertisements may lead to their having a negative self-image and being treated in an offensive way by others – eg speaking slowly and loudly on the assumption that they cannot hear well. In one study one third of those aged 55+

claimed that they did not buy a product because of the stereotyping in the advertisement.

Implications

- Shops can influence budding consumers by providing play facilities, eye-level displays that children can readily see, window displays that they find interesting, sales staff trained to deal with children, and attending to ethical and legal worries of parents, eg not selling tobacco to underage children.
- Advertisements aimed at children can influence requests for products but they need to be memorable for the child (using action, heroes and slogans) and repeated frequently. Humour, novelty, fast pace and careful selection of music, language and images are all essential if they are to appeal to this age group. Care must be taken that the advertisement is not misleading to younger children.
- Products aimed at children need to be thoroughly tested on children to ensure that they are appealing; such testing rejected the idea of a Batman lollipop because children thought that sucking Batman would not be appropriate.
- Older consumers have different interests to younger ones but it is better to focus on their cognitive age rather than their chronological age. Older women who have a younger cognitive age will prefer younger fashions.
- Older consumers need to feel confident about what they purchase and where they purchase it. Relationship marketing may be particularly important with this group, as is providing transport and safe comfortable environments in which to shop. This will

pay off in terms of brand or store loyalty as older people are more loyal customers.

- Encouraging complaints and feedback from this group may be particularly important, given that they will not always complain spontaneously.
- Advertisements aimed at older people are few and far between. They can be effective provided that they avoid stereotyping (ideally avoid portraying older people and focusing instead on the issue concerned) and stress quality, security and independence. Since information is processsed more slowly, the pace of the presentation needs to be slower than that for younger groups. Nostalgia can often be put to good use, as in advertisements for Hovis.
- Product developers need to consult potential users. Heinz blundered by introducing 'senior food' after finding that older people were buying jars of baby food because it did not require chewing. Older people would not buy it because of the image although they continued to buy the baby food!

Social class

Definitions/issues

Social status is position in society relative to others. A social class is a group of individuals who have a similar status. It is measured by a number of indicators including education, occupation and income. In some societies (described as 'open'), movement between classes is easy; in closed societies it is difficult or impossible. It is relevant to consumer behaviour because it indicates both purchasing power and purchasing preferences.

> ### ACTIVITY
>
> Which products and activities would you associate with the upper, middle and working classes?

Important points

1 Certain products, services and stores are associated with particular social classes. Social class seems to be a good predictor of purchasing goods such as cosmetics and alcohol – and items associated with 'taste' such as homes, cars and furnishings. Some items, like Rolex watches, may be bought as indicators of class.

2 Leisure activities also vary according to class. Jogging, swimming and tennis may be favoured by the upper classes and team sports by the lower classes. The middle classes are more likely to use public facilities as the rich have their own (although high-status health clubs and golf clubs are an exception). The lower classes may not be able to afford them at all. Tastes in music and reading material also vary.

3 The reasons for valuing different possessions have been found to vary with class. Sentimental or aesthetic reasons were given by business people far more than by unemployed people, who were more likely to refer to economic value and usefulness.

4 Purchasing can be affected by the desire to 'buy up' into a particular social class. The idea is that by making the right purchases, a person can be accepted as being from a higher social class. The ultimate extension of this idea can be seen in the form of **conspicuous consumption** where wealth is displayed through lavish entertaining or **conspicuous waste** where resources are not properly used or thrown away when still useful.

5 **Parody display** is another way of displaying status. In this case it is done through conspicuous avoidance of status symbols and fashionable items as in the fashion for ex-military vehicles instead of luxury motors.

6 Product information-search varies with social class. The working class may have fewer sources available and may rely more on word of mouth. Particular newspapers and magazines are read by particular social classes as well. Use of language by classes differs, with more complex linguistic forms being used by the upper classes and simpler sentence forms and vocabulary by the lower classes.

Implications

- Analysis of product usage by social class allows the product itself, pricing, advertising and retailing to be adapted to market it appropriately.
- Offering a complete service to those attempting to 'buy up' but unsure of their own taste may well prove

to be successful – eg many home builders now provide a furnishing service.

- Products must be accepted as suitable status symbols and their acceptability reviewed regularly to keep pace with changes in fashion.
- Advertising needs to make it clear which social class the product is aimed at. Working class-oriented advertisements tend to use more slang, powerful imagery rather than words to emphasise physical qualities and uses of the product, and are placed in appropriate publications.

Culture

Definitions/issues

Culture refers to the values, attitudes, ways of communicating and material objects (including works of art and everyday artifacts) shared by a group of people. It is an important source of self-identity and ideas about acceptable behaviour. Within any culture there are also smaller subcultural groups which vary in distinctive ways; these may be regional (as in the different parts of the UK), religious or ethnic. It is essential to understand the values and traditions of different groups if marketing is to be done successfully. This is known as **ethnoconsumerism**.

Important points

1 Culturally appropriate behaviour regarding choice and use of products is embodied in **consumption values**. These dictate the product's function (and consumer expectations of quality), form (eg whether washing machines have to be front or top-loading), and meaning (eg certain food may have religious connotations in some societies).

2 Cultures produce their own myths – often stories about the triumph of good over evil; Superman can be regarded as a modern myth.

3 Cultures also have rituals such as the observance of Christmas Day and birthdays, taking holidays, weddings and gift-giving.

4 Some events, people and objects are given special significance in a culture and are described as being **sacred.** They may then be collected or indulged in for their own sake.

5 Many countries (such as Britain and the USA) are multicultural and need to take account of the sizeable minority group market. African Americans, for example, comprise 12% of the population and have distinctive lifestyles, family structures, dietary practices, fashion preferences and cosmetic needs.

6 Although the core values of a culture remain relatively constant, changes in society are occurring all the time; for example, there are changes in divorce rates and gender roles. Particular generations may also have specific experiences (eg living through a period of social protest) which give them unique characteristics. Political and social conditions can thus lead to certain products being more acceptable than others.

7 Popular culture involves changes in fashion being accepted by large numbers of people at the same time because they express relevant meanings and needs. This can affect a wide range of products from clothing to foods, music, leisure activities, holiday destinations etc. Fashions may be long-lived, in which case they are known as 'classics' (eg court shoes for women) or short-term 'fads' such as yo-yos.

8 Marketing itself is part of modern culture. **Product placement** (paying film and televison producers to include products such as in the use of BMW cars in James Bond films) has become big business. Theme parks represent an extreme form of **reality engineering** where an entire cultural environment is constructed by the marketers.

Implications

- Violation of cultural expectations will have an adverse impact on product success. The Spice Girls did not go down too well in New Zealand when they performed a Maori war dance meant to be performed only by men! In Japan, the word for the number '4' also means death, and Japanese people are very superstitious about buying items in fours.
- Consumption values need to be researched before products are marketed in specific cultures. For example, expensive high-quality washing machines have not proved to be succcessful in the USA although they are sought after in Germany.
- Advertisements based on mythological figures or popular themes (eg the alien from outer space/ET) will be easy for consumers to understand and relate to.
- Rituals can be used to marketing advantage, as in Christmas and birthday presents. Self-gifts ('because you're worth it') can be used to boost sales.
- Items which are sacred take on a value that far exceeds their worth and therefore present a good marketing opportunity. Consider the success of Pokemon cards, for example.
- Using advertisements directed at minority groups could be beneficial where the product is of interest to

them and advertisements are placed in appropriate media.

- Cultural change can indicate important new marketing opportunities eg as family structures and working life have changed, ready meals have become more acceptable to consumers. As well as cultural change the values of different generations need to be taken into account when devising advertising campaigns.
- Marketers have an ethical responsibility to consider the way that products can shape society.

Family and gender roles

Definitions/issues
A family is generally defined as a group of two or more persons who live together and are related by blood, marriage or adoption. A household is a group of persons who share a housing unit and have common housekeeping arrangements. Both groups are important to marketers since they purchase items jointly and influence one another's decisions about what to buy.

Important points
1 A family goes through changes over time: this is known as the **Family Life Cycle (FLC)**. Young couples have children who eventually leave home and the family then consists of two older adults. At each stage there will be changes in income and in expenditure on leisure, food, durables and services according to family requirements. After the birth of a child a young couple may have less money available for leisure activities and for eating out.
2 Family members also have different roles to play in

purchasing decisions. One person may originate an idea and others may provide information, make financial decisions and carry out the purchasing.

ACTIVITY

Think about who makes the purchasing decisions for different types of goods in one household with which you are familiar.

In most families women tend to dominate where groceries and clothing are concerned while men dominate when purchasing hardware and lawnmowers. Holidays, televisions, refrigerators and furniture are joint decisions. Autonomy tends to be the rule for decisions about jewellery, mens' clothing, painting/decorating supplies, luggage, sports equipment and toys/games. Since 1980 consumer research has shown that changes in family structures are leading to changes in gender roles within the family. There is now far more joint decision-making about purchases.

3 Gender roles within the family may also differ; such differences may extend to product preferences (eg men prefer meat and women fruit) and expected behaviours (eg women are traditionally the gift-givers and organisers of social events such as parties). Particular products (such as toys) are often associated with masculinity or femininity (eg Barbie dolls and Action men).

4 The nature of the family has always been variable according to culture; some cultures have extended family units which include grandparents. Recent cultural changes have introduced a variety of new family forms such as

single parents, cohabiting couples, reconstituted families (eg remarried couples with step-children) as well as single-person and multiple-person households.

5 Societal changes in gender roles, based on the rise of feminism and the 'new man', have led to rejection of the sex-typed product by many consumers. The increase in women's employment has created new strains for women who feel they have to cope with two 'jobs'.

New Man   Two Jobs Woman

6 As well as defining the typical behaviours of men and women, society portrays ideal images of how they should look – what is regarded as 'beautiful'. This differs according to culture and era, as shown by the fact that Miss World winners are getting thinner and thinner.

Implications

> • FLC affects consumption and marketers can target different groups accordingly. Alcohol consumption and leisure activities are more relevant to young

couples, child care facilities to those with young children and home maintenance services to older couples.

- Understanding of roles played in decision-making can help marketers to target the correct family member. Decision-makers and buyers may be more important to marketers than users are for some items.

- Advertisers have traditionally portrayed certain gender roles in advertisements and sex-typed their products. As a result of public concern with the effects of such communications, this is no longer acceptable to most consumers. Women are increasingly being portrayed as independent and responsible and men as sharing in domestic work.

- New types of family unit present new opportunities for market segmentation. Gay and lesbian couples, single parents and cohabiting couples and the divorced can all be focused on by advertisers for different purposes. For example, divorced persons may need an entire set of household equipment. Similarly, changing gender roles offer scope for new marketing strategies. Unisex toys, and new depictions of men and women in advertisements are all responses to societal changes which in turn act to socialise the next generation into their roles.

- Ideals of beauty are used by advertisers to heighten the insecurity that many people feel about their appearance and to promote the wish to use particular products to change themselves. Clothing, cosmetics, dietary aids, plastic surgery, body piercing and tattooing are all promoted with this in mind and provide lucrative markets.

Summary

Today we have been looking at different types of consumer and we have seen that:

- Children and the elderly present different types of challenges to marketers
- Social class is associated with differences in product usage and therefore 'buying up' can be encouraged
- An awareness of cultural values and cultural changes is essential for effective product development and marketing
- Marketing opportunities are presented by changing gender roles and different stages of family life

Tomorrow we will be looking at product branding and advertising, to explore how this information can be put to good use.

Sell Your Product I: Branding and Advertising

Today we will be examining the process of communicating with potential consumers. The success of a product is dependent on this and in turn depends on the knowledge about consumers that you have already acquired from previous chapters of this book. We will be looking at:

- Product branding and brand loyalty
- Brand awareness and brand extensions
- Product naming and corporate image
- Advertising
- Direct behaviour shaping

Product branding and brand loyalty

Definitions/issues
A brand is a distinctive name (such as Campbell's soup) and/or symbol (such as a trademark or packaging) which identifies a product and distinguishes it from those produced by competitors. Brand loyalty is the tendency shown by consumers to prefer one brand to another and continue to buy it over a period of time.

ACTIVITY

See if you can think of the logo/trademark of the following companies:
- McDonalds
- Peugeot
- Sure deodorant

- BP
- Labour Party
- Michelin tyres

Important points

1 Each brand has a brand image which refers to the way that consumers think about the product and its properties. This can include quality, status associations, and expectations about other aspects, such as softness and strength in paper handkerchiefs. This image may be an important determinant of purchase.

2 Most people show loyalty to one or multiple brands. 58–65% of purchases tend to be of the first brand across a range of grocery products. Availability, need for variety and special offers generally prevent sole brand loyalty from being the norm.

3 Sole brand loyalty is more common in people who are light purchasers but as they are generally more numerous, they are an important category. They are also more likely to have higher incomes, and are therefore less affected by special discounts.

4 Brand leaders (such as Persil) achieve greater loyalty than other brands, possibly because they advertise more.

Implications

> • Improving brand image by advertising may help to increase sales, provided the consumer can afford and obtain the product concerned. However it has been estimated that consumers may only buy about 4% of what they see advertised. Adverse publicity can harm brand image and reduce sales, as seen when Gerald Ratner described his own jewellery as 'total crap'.

- Good distribution and special offers may be helpful for promoting certain products, such as those where people like variety.
- In other areas sole brand loyalty may be more likely and such purchasers may not need price promotions.
- Money spent on advertising may be recouped especially in the case of brand leaders. This has to be balanced against the increased prices that often result from funding advertising campaigns.

ACTIVITY

Think about your own purchases of a range of groceries, clothing, petrol, etc. Which brands do you buy? Do you change each time or are you loyal? What image do you associate with each brand?

Brand awareness and brand extensions

Important points

1 The extent to which brands are differentiated from one another is known as brand awareness. This may be high (for baked beans) or low (for sugar). When awareness is very high one brand may become synonymous with the category, eg Hellman's has become synonymous with mayonnaise.

2 Some brand names are so popular that they can be used to launch new products or to take over the products of other companies. Sir Richard Branson's 'Virgin' name has been used in just this way.

3 Rather than launching new names it is preferable to use existing brands and extend them to new products: brand extensions. Eg, Persil have extended into different types of washing powder and liquids as well as washing-up liquid.

Implications

- Advertising needs to reinforce the brand name and promote awareness.
- Where brand awareness is weak, advertising may benefit the competition as much as the advertiser. (This was found in the DIY market in Britain in recent years, where advertisements boosted DIY sales across all retailers). Sales promotions and loyalty discounts may be better ways of increasing sales in such circumstances.
- Money spent developing a strong brand name will be repaid when it can be applied to new products as extensions. These must fit in with the range of products with which the brand is already associated

and must be sufficiently different to prevent losses in sales by the existing products.

Product naming and corporate image

Definitions/issues

The name given to a product is sometimes an important determinant of its popularity. Diet Coke did not sell well when it was first launched under the name 'Tab'. The image of the parent company, as exemplified by its logo, may similarly affect how well its products sell.

Important points

1 Brand awareness may well depend on having made a good choice of brand name.
2 The name also needs to be applicable to use in other countries. 'Nova' in Spain implies that a car will not go and the Mitsubishi 'Pajero' translates as 'Wanker'. Wrigley's spearmint gum translates as 'shark's sperm' in some parts of Eastern Europe. Names have to take into account future brand extensions as well – the use of Hotpoint for refrigerators does not seem very applicable!
3 Company names and logos evoke images which may be negative or favourable; if the latter, they may enhance brand loyalty.

Implications

- New brand names need to be distinctive and easy to remember in order to promote brand awareness.
- Brand names need to be chosen carefully with regard to future developments in products and markets.
- Money spent on designing a company logo may be

recouped in sales if it is an appropriate one.
* Research into the image of a company needs to be
  constantly updated to ensure that it is still positive.
  The Prudential Assurance Company found that it
  had become known as 'the Pru', which had negative
  connotations; it then had to change its logo and
  communications to present itself more forcefully as
  the Prudential.

Advertising

Definitions/issues

The process of persuasion involves a source of information
(eg the company which is marketing the product or the
person who appears for them in the advertisement), a
message (eg that butter substitutes are better for your health),
a medium of communication (eg newspapers), and a receiver
(the consumers who interpret the information). Examining
the process in terms of these elements demonstrates that a
variety of factors can influence how persuasive the process is.

ACTIVITY

Think about 4 advertisements that you can recall well.
What has made them memorable?

Important points

1 The effectiveness of the source depends primarily on
  communicator credibility (including expertise and
  trustworthiness) and attractiveness (which can include
  physical appearance as well as status).
2 Messages are more effective if they use both rational and

emotional appeals and avoid excessive use of fear. Sex and humour attract attention but may not improve attitudes towards the product. The way that information is presented and the words used to describe the product (including its name) will influence the way that it is perceived. For example, the colour orange is perceived as cheap, and dark-coloured objects are perceived as heavier than identical ones in lighter colours. Big Mac or Whopper burgers will be perceived as bigger than burgers of an

Big

Supergianthumungousburger

identical size which are described as singles.

3 The nature of the target group will also determine the content of the advertisement; better-educated consumers prefer two-sided arguments and those low in self-esteem will respond to products which offer to increase this.

4 The **elaboration likelihood model** of persuasion suggests that an important factor in advertisement design is the degree of involvement of the consumer with the product. Highly involved consumers will be more influenced by the

message content, and low-involvement consumers by the message source.

5 The nature of the product (whether it is utilitarian or purely for enjoyment, whether it is a new product, what kind of image is desired for it, whether it is better than its competitors) will also influence the nature of the advertisement.

6 Finally, the attention, interest and desire that have been generated by the advertisement need to be translated into action in the form of purchase.

Implications

- It is essential to determine the nature of the target consumer group before an advertising campaign can be mounted since it affects choice of source, message content and medium.
- Use of celebrities can enhance source effectiveness provided that their image and that of the product are well-matched. Gary Lineker's 'Mr Nice Guy' reputation was used appropriately by Walkers to increase awareness of their product from 40 to 60%, for example. On the other hand, Pepsi had to abandon Michael Jackson after he was accused of child abuse. The credibility of celebrities is not always high, especially if they endorse too many products.
- Advertisements need to be carefully designed to interest the target consumers, and will need to be regularly changed to prevent them losing interest.
- Advertisements must take existing levels of knowledge of consumers into account and understanding and interpretation must be checked at an early stage in the campaign; it cannot be

assumed that the perception will be as intended.

- In order to gain acceptance, advertisements must evoke positive thoughts and feelings. Pictures which have this effect – even if irrelevant to the product – can improve acceptance of the product.
- Information which is well organised, repeated, makes good use of visual images, and is relevant to needs will be better remembered.
- Both source and content ('how' and 'what') are important elements of advertising since they appeal to different types of consumer (high vs low involvement).
- Utilitarian products may be better promoted by informational than by emotional appeals. Where there is no clear difference in performance that the advert can capitalise on, sales may be promoted by peripheral cues such as the use of attractive pictures.
- Information needs to be presented using media that will be observed by the target group of consumers eg the 'Sun' or the 'Independent'.
- The product must be readily available and appropriately priced to encourage purchase. Indicating where it can be bought may be a useful part of the advertising process.

Direct behaviour shaping

Definitions/issues
Advertising has limitations in producing behaviour change as there is no guaranteee that consumers will see advertisements or respond to them. Behaviour shaping approaches have therefore been developed which involve requests being made directly to consumers.

Important points

1 Prompts to buy something related can be given when consumers are making a purchase. For example, a waitress in a restaurant may ask consumers if they would like anything to drink with the meal.

2 A large request can be preceded by a smaller one (known as the 'foot-in-the-door' technique). Research has shown that asking homeowners to display a large road safety sign in their gardens was successful only 17% of the time; if they were asked first of all to display a smaller poster in the window on the same theme, 76% agreed to the larger request when it was made later.

3 The 'door-in-the-face' technique involves making an initial large request in the hope that a smaller one will then prove to be more acceptable – which it generally is.

4 Reciprocity is the idea that if a consumer is given something as a gift they will then feel obliged to reciprocate by making a purchase.

5 Making a public commitment to an action has been found

to increase the chances that people will stick to it. This can apply to agreeing to give something a try or to writing something down for future reference.

6 Incentives can be used to increase purchases or interest in the product. Coupons have been found to lead to double the number of purchases in households which received them compared with no-coupon households. Price discounts and competitions are other incentive schemes.

Implications

- Prompts can be an effective way of encouraging consumers to consider purchases they may otherwise have overlooked.
- The foot-in-the-door technique is generally more effective than a simple request though its effectiveness is dependent on the amount of time delay between the two requests, the similarity of the two requests and whether or not the first one is actually carried out in practice.
- Door-in-the-face is used by sales staff to encourage more expensive purchases, by offering the top of the range products first and then working down to the lower. The average sale has been found to be considerably more than if the reverse is done.
- Offering tasters of foods in supermarkets can lead to consumers feeling obliged to make purchases; similarly charities often include free gifts (such as pens) in letters requesting donations.
- If consumers fill in agreement forms themselves they are more likely to feel committed to the purchase. Research has shown that they are then less likely to cancel the agreement.

- Although incentives increase purchases, they are costly and may therefore be unwise unless the increased sales compensate for the reduced profits on each sale. Consumers may also become so used to incentives that they will not purchase without them. Ford cars tried to remove incentives only to find that sales fell dramatically, obliging them to reintroduce the schemes.

Summary

Today you have seen that:

- A good brand image is important and can enhance brand loyalty for some types of product.
- Advertising can promote brand awareness and increase the strength of the brand name.
- Brand names and corporate logos need to be carefully chosen and regularly checked for acceptability.
- Message content and source are equally important when designing advertisements and must be tailored to the product and the target consumer.
- Advertising may often need to be supplemented by direct requests and offers in order to bring about behaviour change.

Tomorrow we shall move on to retailing which is hopefully the final stage of selling your product.

Sell Your Product II: Retailing

Today we will be looking at the process of matching consumers with products so that purchases can be made. Even when they have decided to make a purchase, consumers may be put off if there are obstacles in their way, so anything that can be done to make the shopping process easier will obviously boost sales. Important areas to consider include:

- Shoppers
- Store preferences
- Store loyalty
- Shopping locations and shopping trends

Shoppers

Definitions/issues

It is important to consider the reasons why people go shopping and the influences on them when they do shop. If the retail environment can be set up to appeal to their needs more fully, they may be encouraged to spend more time there and/or spend more money during their trip.

ACTIVITY

How much time each week do you spend shopping? How many trips do you make? Why do you go shopping?

Important points

1 People are spending less time shopping than they used to. Most make one main trip each week – often on the same

day – and sometimes secondary trips. Shopping no longer rates as a popular leisure activity having been replaced by relaxing at home, spending time with families and outdoor activities.

2 Several different shopping types have been identified including economic consumers (concern with value), personalised consumers (concern with relationships), ethical consumers (wanting to help the underdog), recreational shoppers (shopping as a leisure activity) and apathetic consumers (who dislike shopping).

3 Frequent shoppers are motivated by personal motives such as dispelling boredom, beating the system, relieving depression and fulfilling fantasies as well as social motives such as alleviating loneliness and providing for others.

4 The number and type of other shoppers in a retail outlet influences the way shoppers see their surroundings and how they feel. Places which are too crowded or too empty are generally unpopular. Crowding in particular reduces shopping time, non-essential purchases and interaction with sales staff, and generally leads to a negative evaluation of the shopping experience. The appearance of other shoppers gives important clues to the status of the establishment.

5 Lack of time is expressed by many shoppers as a problem; however, this may be a matter of perception since modern society has more time free of work and housework than ever before.

6 People who are stimulated or aroused and have pleasant experiences will be in a better mood and evaluate goods and services more positively. Shopping is not just a utilitarian exercise.

Implications

- As time for shopping is limited to one weekly trip in many cases, goods and services must be available from a fairly compact area. If it can be made family-friendly and relaxing, shoppers may be able to combine their needs to spend time with families and relax with shopping. Many supermarkets now have cafes and children's areas for this reason.
- Retail outlets need to cater for a range of motives as well as simply providing products and services. This includes giving good value, doing so in an ethical way, providing a personal touch and creating an enjoyable leisure experience.
- Design of the retail area can go a long way towards reducing the impression of crowding; high ceilings create a feeling of spaciousness. Offering discounts at off-peak times (at the beginning of the week, around lunch-times and in the afternoon) or simply advertising so that consumers know when those quiet times are, may also reduce crowding.
- For some types of product or service it may be necessary to restrict access to consumers who have the right appearance. Hence many restaurants and clubs will have dress codes.
- Time spent waiting in queues needs to be reduced. This can be done by changing the layout of the outlet as in an airport where baggage reclaims were moved further away, making travellers spend more time walking but less time queueing. Or it can be done by providing a diversion, such as a mirror placed by a lift, which decreases reported waiting times.

- Happy music, attention to store design (including colour, smells, etc) and cheerful staff can be used to improve mood and hence evaluation of products.

Store preferences

Definitions/issues

Since most consumers will visit a limited range of shops, it is important to identify what determines their choices. Choice and design of outlet from which to sell products has become a key feature of successful marketing. It has been found that a store can improve its sales by up to 300% by changing colours, lighting and signs.

ACTIVITY

Which stores do you prefer to shop in and why?

Important points

1 Availability of information about products may influence preference; if it is readily available, in an easily understandable form, consumers will be more likely to make use of the store.

2 Music contributes considerably to store atmospherics. Slow music increases both shopping time and expenditure, compared to fast music. Loud music reduces shopping time but not expenditure.

3 Layout of stores can be manipulated to ensure that consumers can move around the store easily (even when other shoppers and trolleys may be around) and to ensure that they come into contact with particular products.

4 Studies of the effects of colour are not always reliable, but it has been suggested that using bright, warm colours outside helps to draw consumers in. Inside, cool colours like blue and green may be more relaxing. Green in particular may be calming where queueing takes place and red may stimulate impulse-buying and perceptions that goods are up-to-date.

5 Stores are also chosen for their image which represents a general view about the range, quality, value and service that the store provides.

6 Other important determinants of supermarket preference have been found to be cleanliness, well-stocked shelves, range of products, number of checkouts, helpful staff, disabled access, wide aisles, car parking, range of different checkouts (eg express), free bags and environmentally friendly goods.

Implications

- Information must be available in the appropriate form. Consumers prefer number ratings or figures (e.g 30mpg) to written evaluation (excellent, good, etc).

- Choice of music needs to be adapted to the nature of the store; where consumers need to be encouraged to pass through quickly, louder music may be beneficial. Music can be used to manipulate perceptions of the store's image – classical music may give the store a more up-market image and has been found to be associated with the purchase of more expensive wines when played in a wine store. Music also needs to be matched to the demographic characteristics of the consumers as can be seen in fashion shops. Studies have shown that when it is, shopping time and purchases can rise by around 18%.

- Placing bakery departments near entrances to provide good smells and impulse buy products near the check-outs are two examples of how location can be utilised within-store to promote purchases. Areas where a lot of people will pass (eg the ends of aisles) can be used for special promotions. Placing popular lines – such as the delicatessen – at the back of the store means that people will have to go past all of the other products in order to reach them.

- Cueing can be done by placing products near those that they may be associated with eg placing dips near crisps. Items at eye level sell twice as well as those at low levels.

- Although the effects are more variable, the colour of both the exterior and the interior of a store needs careful thought. The general colour scheme may contribute to store image but it may also be

necessary to change the colour in different parts of the store. As well as colour, materials used can convey particular impressions; Laura Ashley use wood to convey quality and solidity. Aromas can also be used, as they are in the Body Shop.

- Because the image of a store is slow to change, it is important to make use of corporate advertising to ensure that this is a good one. Tesco are still thought of as relatively cheap and cheerful despite having improved their range of products in recent years.
- Consumer surveys indicate that a wide range of features to do with the social and physical aspects of the store need to be considered when trying to increase the store's share of the market.

Store loyalty

Definitions/issues
Store loyalty is usually defined as the proportion of
expenditure that occurs in the store most used for any
particular type of purchase. This need not necessarily be the
largest proportion – it is possible to spend more money in a
store that is less often used. Therefore it is important to
understand the reasons for store loyalty.

Important points
1 Levels of loyalty appear to be quite high – around 75%
   over one month and 65% over a year for supermarkets.
   75% of expenditure occurs in the favourite store.
2 Store loyalty may be the outcome of limited resources in
   terms of choice, time, transport or money, or it may simply
   reflect lack of interest in shopping around.
3 High loyalty is most common in the 25–44 age group,
   particularly where there are several school age children in
   the family and the mother works. This indicates that loyalty
   may be a form of efficiency reflecting a preference for 'one-
   stop' shopping in those people who have busy lives.

Implications

- Since loyalty levels are generally quite high it would
  seem to be the preferred way to shop where the right
  stores are available.
- High loyalty shoppers have been shown to spend up
  to 70% more in their preferred store than low loyalty
  shoppers, making them useful people to recruit.
- Increasing the efficiency with which shopping can be
  carried out may well appeal to high loyalty shoppers
  and encourage them to use the store.

> • Loyalty cards have been introduced by many stores to try to keep customers, offering dividends or discounts in return for repeated purchases. Sainsbury's managed to increase their share of the market by 1% following the introduction of such a card.

Shopping locations and shopping trends

Definitions/issues
Shopping has changed a great deal in recent years – in terms of both where the main shops are located in a town or city and what kind of shops there are. There have also been changes in the method of retailing so that shopping can be done through other channels. These changes can have implications for marketers as well as for consumers.

Important points
1 Location is a key determinant of store preference and can affect sales dramatically. Eg, McDonald's makes twice as many sales as its two main rivals combined.
2 Out-of-town shopping complexes, such as Lakeside and Bluewater, offer easy parking and a large number of different retail outlets, as well as entertainment centres and recreational facilities. They have proved to be popular with shoppers who see shopping as a leisure activity.
3 City-centre shopping is often concentrated in shopping malls. The largest of these is the West Edmonton Mall in Canada which has 800 stores, 19 cinemas, a hotel, 110 food outlets, a 5-acre indoor waterpark, a golf course, a chapel and a zoo. These pedestrianised zones tend to have a large number of smaller specialist shops such as newsagents.
4 Mail order shopping has changed from providing cheap fashion and household goods on credit to the working

classes to selling a wide range of specialist and high-quality goods (eg Laura Ashley's 'Home' catalogue) to the middle and upper classes. The availability of credit cards, telephones and the internet has boosted this type of retailing in recent years.

5 Internet shopping is particularly popular with younger shoppers (in their teens and twenties). Danish figures for the year 2000 estimated that 60% of companies would have a website and 20% of households internet access.

Implications

- When planning to expand into new locations it is important to analyse the demographic characteristics of the consumers in that area as well as the competition from other retailers. This is known as market selection and should help to identify key cities that could be targeted. Then area analysis can be carried out to narrow down the choice to certain areas within those cities. Finally choice of specific site can be made based on size, cost, parking, public transport, ease of access, visibility, etc. A few hundred yards difference can be crucial in determining the success of the store.
- Very large complexes and stores can suffer from impersonality, and loyalty may be reduced because of this. Therefore it is all the more important to emphasise the relationship aspects of selling when training staff.
- Leisure facilities are essential in some types of outlet but will not be cost-effective in others, as shoppers are there for functional reasons only.
- Smaller shops may be making a come-back.

Planning authorities are now less prepared to give permission for out-of-town stores because city centres are becoming deserted. Smaller local shops are also more convenient and personal. Hence Sainsbury's have introduced the 'Sainsbury's Local', a smaller version shop with a good range of popular items that remains open for long hours.

Sainsburys

This is your friendly local mini hypermarket

- Many retailers are trying out a variety of retail forms so that they do not lose customers to the new non-store retailers. Next have mail order and internet strategies as well as their own shops.
- Solving the problems of internet shopping (eg lack of security) is an important issue. However it requires consumers to take the initiative and many still prefer the experience of visiting shops.

Summary

Today we have seen that:

- Shoppers are motivated by pleasure and practicality; stores must cater for both aspects of the shopping experience.
- Shoppers also prefer stores that have a particular image and are influenced by physical aspects of the environment such as layout, design, music, smells and form in which information is presented.
- Encouraging store loyalty boosts sales a great deal.
- Careful consideration also needs to be given to store size and location as well as alternative retailing strategies.

Tomorrow we will finish our exploration of consumer behaviour by looking at some of the negative effects of a 'consumer society'.

Negative Effects and Implications

Today we are going to look at difficulties that may arise as a result of living in a consumer society and being subjected to some of the marketing strategies we have been discussing. This chapter is divided into three sections, as follows:

- Individual effects
- Environmental effects
- Socio-cultural effects

Individual effects

Definitions/issues

Encouraging consumption may have detrimental consequences for individuals which can lead to behaviour disorders. Consumption can become a compulsion, often carried out in order to boost the self-esteem of the person concerned. It becomes disruptive both socially and financially and is associated with guilt and depression. In this section we will consider the following: compulsive shopping, hoarding and collecting; shoplifting and kleptomania; gambling; eating disorders; and other disorders of body image.

Important points

1 Compulsive shoppers ('shopaholics') are driven by the impulse to buy; in many cases they never use the things that they acquire. It has been estimated that 15 million Americans may be compulsive shoppers. Up to 92% of

these may be younger women who have problems with self-esteem and disturbed relationships with partners. Those with partners who work excessively, control or ignore them, are more likely to be compulsive shoppers. Making purchases lifts their mood temporarily.

2 Collecting and hoarding behaviour differs from compulsive shopping in that it is the objects themselves that are valued, not the act of purchase. It has been reported that two-thirds of American households have collections of some kind. It is problematic when it becomes single-minded, when debts are incurred and when space becomes limited because sufferers refuse to part with anything, even old newspapers. This in turn impairs social life because they cannot receive visitors.

3 Shoplifting occurs in as many as 5% of shoppers at some point in time – though up to 50% of thefts from shops are in fact carried out by staff. Having open shelves (as in supermarkets) promotes sales and reduces the need for staff but promotes shoplifting. Although traditionally seen as a female behaviour, most shoplifters in recent years have been males aged 10–18. It may be done for gain and excitement (particularly in poorer groups) or it may be associated with depression (especially likely in isolated or bereaved women), or the absent-mindedness associated with early dementia.

4 **Kleptomania** is defined as repeated failure to resist impulses to steal objects that are not required for personal use or for monetary gain. The items stolen may even be thrown away. The act of stealing provides a momentary thrill that relieves tension. Fewer than 5% of arrested shoplifters have this disorder and it is more prevalent in females. Relationships, both childhood and marital, are often unhappy.

John is training to be a shoplifter

5 Pathological gambling occurs when people become unable to resist the impulse to gamble despite often being financially ruined. In America, it has been estimated to affect 3% of the adult population, most of whom are men. Heavy lottery players have been found to be low income but with high levels of fantasy about winning. Gamblers may also be motivated by the excitement associated with taking risks, and may be prone to mood disorders.

6 The gambling situation is also set up to increase gambling behaviour: advertising levels are high (eg National Lottery and scratchcards); the behaviour is quick to carry out (some American states have lottery draws every hour); it can be repeated as often as the gambler can afford to do it (eg scratchcards); payouts are large and unpredictable; and many near misses are built into the system (eg with fruit machines). Casinos often have minimum bets, low light levels and no clocks so that people lose track of time, stay longer and spend more.

7 Motivating consumers to aspire to an ideal physical

appearance can lead to a variety of mental disorders. The most obvious of these are the eating disorders anorexia nervosa and bulimia nervosa. Anorexics are mainly young girls (as many as 90% of whom report being dissatisfied with their weight) and they have a perception of themselves as being overweight which leads them to starve themselves. Bulimics are not neccessarily underweight but are prone to massive food binges (up to 5000 calories) followed by guilt and purging in the form of induced vomiting or use of laxatives. This can lead to physical problems such as constipation, or even burst stomachs, and to social isolation as a result of their guilt feelings and the cost of all the food needed to maintain the behaviour.

8 Bodily dysmorphophobia is a general term for body image distortions. Sufferers may feel that their breasts are too small or their noses too large though objectively they are normal. This may lead to their seeking plastic surgery (which can in itself be hazardous, as in silicone breast implants), or to self-mutilation.

Implications

- Therapy for compulsive shopping, hoarding and collecting starts with investigating upbringing and attitudes to money and possessions, followed by an examination of the functions that the behaviour serves at present for the client. Changes in lifestyles and self-concept may be necessary to reduce these needs.
- Surveillance of open shelves is particularly important and most shops now have CCTV and store detectives. Limiting the number of young people allowed in a shop at one time has also been used as

a way of increasing their visibility to staff. Most shoplifters are unlikely to re-offend and would benefit from therapeutic interventions to treat their emotional problems which courts will often arrange.

- Very little has been done to assist people with kleptomania as it is rarely seen. It may respond to treatment with antidepressant drugs such as Prozac and to psychotherapy.
- Gamblers require psychotherapy to treat their problems. They may need to develop other outlets for their need for excitement, and family problems will also need to be dealt with. It has been suggested that organisations such as Camelot should be required to fund treatment centres.
- Regulation of gambling can also be achieved through restriction of advertising, reducing the number of outlets and locating them away from vulnerable members of the populace. The frequency of lottery draws can also be reduced so that there is less chance of habits forming.
- Disorders of bodily image have been blamed on the excessive use of advertising that promotes unattainable ideals, especially for young women, and the use of extremely thin models. Recently, advertisers and fashion houses have been encouraged to use women who are average-sized, and there have been more campaigns in support of fat people.
- Many people who suffer from disorders of body image have other difficulties, such as low self-esteem, depression and family problems which have been found to respond to treatment using antidepressant drugs and psychotherapy.

Environmental effects

Definitions/issues

The relationship between people and the environment they inhabit is a complex one and it has many implications for consumer behaviour. Consumption of resources and disposal of waste are key issues. The attitudes of consumers have changed in recent years with respect to green issues and health, affecting their choice of products and their attitudes towards the companies that manufacture them.

Important points

1 Private households, industry and service/commercial users contribute roughly equally to energy consumption which in turn depletes resources and adds to the greenhouse effect and pollution levels.

2 A typical American has been estimated to generate 25lb of solid waste in a week. This causes problems when considering where to dispose of it – landfill sites, incinerators, disposal at sea and littering being the obvious choices. Not only is this dangerous and polluting, it simply adds to the problem of inadequate resources.

3 As many as 80% of consumers – 'green consumers' – want to buy environmentally responsible products. In the UK, around 10% of these are heavily committed to doing so. This extends to the means of production (is the company responsible for pollution?), resources used (is timber from sustainable forests?), packaging (is it recyclable?), product development (is it tested on animals?), and effects on health of consumers.

ACTIVITY

What do you feel about environmental issues? Give yourself a rating on a scale from 1 (not at all interested) to 10 (very concerned). Now think about your shopping behaviour. Do concerns about the environment affect your product choices? Does this fit in with your general level of concern for the environment as noted above? If there is a discrepancy, why do you think this is?

Implications

- Consumers can be encouraged to use products which are themselves energy-saving. For example, it has been estimated that in 1970, if the most efficient refrigerator had been chosen by all purchasers in the USA, 17 million tons of coal and 26,000 acres of land from which it would have been mined could have been saved. At some point it may even be

necessary to consider demarketing of some products
– encouraging consumers to buy them less often if at
all – the motor car being the obvious example.

- Littering (disposing of waste in the wrong place) can
be reduced by around 15% by the provision of more
bins on the street; these are most effective if they
are bright and colourful. A more direct way of
reducing littering would be to reduce the excess
packaging of products or offer incentives for
disposing of it correctly.

- The amount of waste generated can also be reduced
by introducing recycling (recovery of materials, as in
bottle banks), re-use (using things for different
purposes as in the use of worn tyres for sileage
clamps), remarketing (eg second hand sales), and
reclamation (remanufacture of materials eg making
plastic drinks bottles into insulation). Some
manufacturers, such as BMW, have introduced
incentives for recycling components from their cars.
The easier it is made for consumers to comply with
such schemes, the more likely it is that they will do so.

- Green concerns present new marketing
opportunities. The Belgian company Ecover has
produced a range of cleaning products which are
enzyme and phosphate-free; CFC-free pump-action
sprays; and Body Shop cosmetics are all products
designed with the environment in mind. Recent food
products which cater for consumers' health concerns
include vegetarian and organic foods, sugar, salt and
fat-free foods and alcohol-free beers and wines.

- Some companies have responded to environmental
concerns by representing themselves as green: BP

has now presented a new image of being 'Beyond Petroleum'.

Social/cultural effects

Definitions/issues

Consumer rights have been an issue since early campaigners (such as Ralph Nader in 1950s America) first made people aware that they were not always being treated ethically by companies. With the rise of global marketing in recent years, it has now extended to ethical concerns about the way that companies behave in other parts of the world.

Important points

1 Consumer rights in America include: the right to safety; to be (accurately) informed; to have a choice of products; to be heard (redress); to enjoy a healthy environment; and (for minority groups) to have their interests protected.

2 In the UK similar rights are upheld by the Office of Fair Trading, the Health and Safety Executive, the Consumer Association and the Advertising Standards Authority.

3 The rights of children has become a particular issue in recent years as children are felt to be more persuadable and more companies are targeting child consumers. There is also concern about the amount of conflict between parent and child that may be promoted by child-focused advertising.

4 Finally, given that people in the West seem to be suffering from increasing levels of unhappiness due to the erosion of community and family life, it has been suggested that marketing our life-style to other cultures may be ethically unsound.

Implications

- Product safety is a major issue and products which are unsafe – such as DDT, some children's toys and certain vehicles – have been withdrawn from the market or recalled for expensive modifications. Other products which raise health concerns – such as silicone breast implants and cigarettes – may go unnoticed for many years but eventually result in costly legal action against the company.
- Labelling of products, listing ingredients and identifying additives and sell-by dates for foods, has now become mandatory. Provision of accurate information extends to advertising, which is required to be 'honest'. Deception is difficult to prove, given that material is often misunderstood by consumers anyway. Volvo cars in North America have been reported for using reinforcement in the cars used for crash tests in their advertisements. Cosmetic surgery clinics have recently been ordered not to play down the risks of surgery in their advertisements and not to claim to be 'leading' establishments unless they have some evidence to back this up.
- The right to choice of products means that companies cannot be allowed to develop monopolies. Education about how to make choices has been advocated in order to improve the quality of choices made by consumers.
- The right to redress means that many more products are accompanied by guarantees these days.
- In 1996, the Advertising Standards Authority in the UK received 12,055 complaints about

advertisements. Of these, 846 were complaints about the sexist portrayal of women, which is more than double the number in the previous year. In 17 cases the adverts were withdrawn. Sexist portrayal of men has also been criticised as in the Micra 'Ask before you borrow it' advert which portrays a man clutching his crotch after taking his wife's car without permission. Another example is the Wallis 'Dressed to kill' slogan showing women distracting male motorists so that they have fatal accidents.

- The extent to which global marketing should show respect for the customs of other cultures needs to be carefully considered. Producers of the TV programme 'Blind Date' were subjected to death threats from Muslim fundamentalists when the programme was exported to Turkey.
- On a more sinister level some tobacco companies are now concentrating their sales drives on Third World countries where awareness of the dangers is less and there are fewer restriction on sales (eg to children).

Summary

In this final chapter we have seen that:

- Encouraging excessive consumption and conveying particular images of the ideal person can affect some individuals detrimentally in the form of compulsive shopping, hoarding, shoplifting, kleptomania, eating disorders and bodily dysmorphophobia.
- Such individuals often have problems with self-esteem and relationships, and need psychotherapy.

- Environmental issues can be addressed by encouraging conservation, use of energy-saving products and recycling, reuse and remarketing.
- Green consumers present new marketing opportunities but also demand environmentally responsible behaviours from companies.
- The rights of consumers to safety, information, choice, redress and a healthy environment must be met.
- The rights of minority groups and members of other cultures must also be respected.

This brief survey of consumer behaviour has attempted to introduce you to some of the key areas of interest to researchers and practitioners as well as addressing the concerns of consumers themselves. Whether you are a consumer or a practitioner, hopefully you have found some areas of interest to stimulate your thoughts, your reading and your behaviours.